KU-242-805

B. A. STARD

Illustrations by
Rob Smith

summersdale

REALLY RUDE JOKES

Copyright © Summersdale Publishers Ltd, 2005

Condition of Sale
This book is sold subject to the condition that it
shall not, by way of trade or otherwise, be lent, re-
sold, hired out or otherwise circulated in any form
of binding or cover other than that in which it is
published and without a similar condition including
this condition being imposed on the subsequent
publisher.

Summersdale Publishers Ltd
46 West Street
Chichester
West Sussex
PO19 1RP
UK

www.summersdale.com

Printed and bound in Great Britain

ISBN 1 84024 460 7

REALLY

Rude Jokes

CONTENTS

SEXUAL HARASSMENT

A young woman storms into her supervisor's office one day and insists on filing a **sexual harassment** suit against a co-worker.

'I'm so tired of his behaviour,' she says. Every day, he walks up to me and, standing really close, he takes a deep breath and then tells me that my **hair smells nice**.'

'That doesn't sound like sexual harassment,' says the supervisor, **puzzled** by her vehemence. 'What's wrong with a co-worker telling you your hair smells nice?'

The woman replies, 'He's a dwarf.'

GRANNY PROSTITUTE

A young prostitute has tried to keep her profession a secret from her family.

One day, the red light district she works in is raided by the police and all the prostitutes are made to line up, including the girl. Suddenly she **spots her grandmother** walking towards the line but there is nowhere to hide.

'Hello, dear,' Grandma says. 'What are you all lining up for?'

Desperate to keep the **truth hidden**, the girl tells her grandmother that she and the other girls are lining up for free oranges that some people are giving away.

Grandma loves oranges so she goes to the end of the queue.

A policeman is questioning each of the prostitutes. He is a little surprised when he reaches Grandma, and asks her, 'You are so old, **how do you do it?**' Grandma replies, 'It's not so difficult. I just take my false teeth out and suck them dry.'

What did one of the blonde's legs say to the other one?

Between you and me we could make a lot of money.

SMART-ARSE

A secondary school teacher reminds her students of the next day's final English exam. 'Now, I might consider a **nuclear attack** or a serious personal injury or illness or a death in your immediate family as an excuse for missing tomorrow's exam, but it's not a certainty and those are the only excuses I'll even think about!'

'What would you say if tomorrow I said I was suffering from complete and utter **sexual exhaustion?**' asks the smart-arse student at the back of the class. All the students struggle unsuccessfully to hide their giggles.

The teacher waits until the laughter has subsided and then smiles **sympathetically** at the student. 'I suppose you'd just have to write your answers with your other hand, then.'

THE WHORE AND HER TAX RETURNS

An accountant is taking details from a new client. After writing down her name and address he asks, 'And **what's your occupation?**'

The woman looks at him and then replies, 'I'm a whore.'

A little surprised, the accountant insists that she'll have to rephrase her occupation to appear less crass.

'How about if I say I'm a **prostitute?**'

'No, you'll have to think of something else. That's still too crude.'

After thinking for a few minutes, the woman states, 'I'm a **chicken farmer.**'

'What does chicken farming have to do with being a prostitute?' asks the bemused accountant. 'Well, I raised over **five thousand** cocks last year.'

BIOLOGY LESSONS

Miss Baker asks Jessica: 'What part of the **human body** increases to ten times its normal size when excited?'

'**That's disgusting!**' Jessica exclaims. 'I won't answer that question!'

Miss Baker then asks little Stephanie, who responds correctly; 'The pupil of the eye.'

Turning to Jessica, Miss Baker says, 'I've three things to say to you, young lady. First, you didn't do your homework; second, you have a **dirty mind**; and third, you're going to be very disappointed!'

THE NEW SECRETARY

A young woman has just started a **new job** as a secretary and is setting up her boss's computer. She goes through the set-up procedure and then asks him for a password.

Feeling a bit smug and wanting to **embarrass her** on her first day, he grins and then tells her to enter '*penis*'. Without batting an eyelid, she enters the password and then bursts out **laughing** at the computer's response: **PASSWORD REJECTED. NOT LONG ENOUGH.**

SCHOOL BLACKBOARD

One morning an attractive teacher walks into her classroom and notices that someone has written the word penis in tiny letters on one corner of the **blackboard**. She quickly scans the class looking for a guilty face. Finding none, she rubs the word off and begins the lesson.

The next day, the word penis is written on the board again but this time it's written in **slightly larger** letters about halfway across the board. Again she looks for the culprit but has to proceed with the day's lesson after rubbing the word away.

Every day the word is on the blackboard in progressively larger letters, and **every day** the teacher vigorously rubs the word away. After several days she walks into the classroom expecting to see the same word written yet again on the blackboard but is instead **greeted** by this message: 'The more you rub it, the bigger it gets.'

WHAT A CHEMIST HEARS

A sixteen-year-old boy walks into the chemist's looking for some condoms.

'Aren't you a bit young to be **needing condoms?**' asks the chemist. 'Why do you want them?'

'Well, I've been seeing this girl for a while now and things are getting hotter, so tonight I'm going to her house to have **dinner with her parents** and after that I'm going to take her upstairs and screw her in every position you can imagine.' The chemist sells the boy the condoms and off he goes.

That night he arrives at his girlfriend's house and she brings him to the dining room to meet her parents. The boy sits at the table, **covers his face** with his hands and starts saying grace. After sitting in silence for five minutes his girlfriend leans over and whispers, 'I didn't realise that you were so **religious**.'

'I didn't realise that your father was a chemist,' the boy replies.

SEX SHOP

A man takes a job in a sex shop. At about noon on his first day, the boss says to his new employee, 'I'm going **out for lunch** now. Let me just remind you of the prices so that you don't lose me any money. Now this is our nine inch pink dildo. It's fifteen pounds.'

The new guy repeats, 'Nine inch pink, fifteen quid. Got it.'

'This is the eleven inch blue dildo. It's twenty-five pounds.'

'Eleven inch blue, twenty-five quid. Got it.'

The boss is **satisfied** and goes to lunch. Shortly after, a very elegant-looking woman walks in. 'How much is that dildo over there?' she asks.

'Ah, that's our nine inch pink dildo. That costs fifteen pounds.'

'What about that blue one there?'

'That's our eleven inch blue. It sells for twenty-five pounds.'

'And how much for **the plaid one** over there?'

'The twelve inch plaid dildo is... fifty pounds.'

The woman looks at the selection again, and decides to buy the plaid one. The man wraps it for her, rings up the sale and she leaves.

A little later, the boss comes **back from lunch**. 'So, how did you do?' he asks.

'Great! I got fifty quid for my thermos!'

LAY OFF

Mr Draper owns a small business and has two employees working for him called Natasha and Jack. Both are extremely **good workers**, always willing to do overtime and go the extra mile when needed.

But one day Mr Draper is looking over his books and sees that he isn't making enough money to keep both of them on; he will have to **lay one off** This is a very **hard decision** as they are both such good employees and he wants to find a fair way of choosing. Eventually he decides to watch them work and whoever takes a break would be the one to go.

So from his office he watches them working. Suddenly, Natasha gets **a splitting headache** She takes some aspirin out of her purse and goes to the water cooler to get a drink. Mr Draper follows her to the water cooler and with a heavy heart says, 'Natasha, I'm going to have to lay you or Jack off.'

Natasha says, 'Can you jack off? I have a headache.'

A brunette, a blonde and a redhead are all in Year Seven at school. Who has the biggest tits?

The blonde, because she's 18.

A WOMAN'S WORK

A man gets into a lift and pushes the button for the fifth floor. Just as he's about to step out of the lift, a **beautiful woman** walks in and, smiling seductively, begins to unbutton her blouse. The man is so **confused** that he doesn't know where to look.

The woman takes off her blouse and throws it on the floor, making the man even more nervous.

Then she takes **off her bra**, throws it on the floor and says, 'Make me feel like a woman.'

He takes **off his shirt**, throws it on the floor and replies, 'All right – iron that.'

PILOT TALK

After a long and tiring flight, the pilot addresses his passengers for the final time. 'Ladies and gentlemen. This is **Captain Johnson** speaking. We're on our final descent into Heathrow Airport. I want to thank you for flying with us today, and I hope you enjoy your stay in London.'

He then carries on his conversation **with his co-pilot**, unaware that he's forgotten to turn the intercom off.

The co-pilot asks, 'Well, Captain, what are your plans for London?'

'First,' says the Captain, 'I'm gonna check into the hotel and take a **nice, long shit**. Then I'm taking that new stewardess out for dinner. You know, the one with the huge hooters. And after wining and dining her, I'm going to take her back to my room and fuck her brains out all night long.'

Her **face burning**, the new stewardess runs to the cockpit to turn off the intercom. On the way, she falls over an old lady's bag and lands flat **on her face**. The old lady turns to her and says quietly, 'There's no need to run, dear. He wants to take a shit first.'

BEASTLY LESSON

One day Miss Jones decides to play an animal game. Holding up a picture of a giraffe, she asks if anyone knows what it is. But nobody raises their hand.

'See its long neck? What animal has a **long neck?**'

Jenny holds up her hand and asks if it is a giraffe.

'Very good, Jenny,' Miss Jones smiles. Next she holds up a picture of a **zebra** and again nobody seems to know what it is. 'See the

stripes on this animal? What animal has stripes?'

Peter holds up his hand and says it is a zebra.

'Very good, Peter. Now what do you think this animal is?' she asks, holding up a picture of a deer. 'See the **big antlers** on this animal. What animal has horns like this?'

But nobody knows.

'Let me give you another hint,' she tries. 'It's something your mother calls your father.'

'I know what it is,' Simon yells **triumphantly**. 'It's a horny bastard.'

IMPROPER PROPOSAL

An ugly but smartly-dressed man approaches a beautiful woman in a bar.

'If I offered you a **million pounds** would you sleep with me?' he asks her.

She takes a moment to think about it and then says, 'Yes – for a million pounds, I **would sleep with you**.'

The ugly man then asks, 'How about for fifty pence?'

The woman is **insulted**. 'What kind of woman do you think I am?'

'Well,' the man says, 'we have established that. Now we're just haggling over the price.'

THE TAXI DRIVER AND THE HOOKER

A taxi driver is driving around London one night. It's grey and dull and rainy, when all of a sudden he spots an arm waving from the dark entrance of an alley.

He pulls up to the curb and **a figure jumps** into the taxi and slams the door.

Looking in his rear view mirror, he's shocked to see a dripping wet, **naked woman** sitting in the back seat.

'Where would you like to go, miss?' he stammers.

'Kings Cross, please,' replies the woman.

'No problem,' he says, taking another long glance in the mirror.

The woman catches him staring at her and demands angrily, 'Just **what the hell** are you looking at?'

'Well, miss,' he answers, 'I can't quite figure out how you're going to pay your fare.'

The woman smiles, then spreads her legs and puts her feet up on the front seat. 'Take your fare out of this.'

Still looking in the mirror, the driver asks, 'Do you have anything smaller?'

THE SWEDISH STUDENT

Two students are dancing in a club, an American guy and a Swedish girl. During a slow song, he gives her a **little squeeze** and says, 'In America, we call this a hug.'

She replies, 'Yaah – in Sveden, we call it a hug too.'

A little while later, he gives **her a peck** on the cheek and says, 'In America, this is called a kiss.'

She replies, 'Yaah – in Sveden, it is called a kiss too.'

It's late at night and they have both had **a lot to drink** when the American guy takes the Swedish girl out to a nearby park and has sex with her.

'In America,' he says, 'we call this a grass sandwich.'

She replies, 'Yaah – in Sveden, we call it a **grass sandwich** too, but we usually put more meat in it.'

THE STUDY OF HARD WORDS

A blonde, redhead and brunette are looking in a **dictionary** for the **hardest** words they can find.

The **brunette's** word is quizzical.

The **redhead's** word is photosynthesis.

The **blonde's** word is dick.

THE DEVIL'S WORK

A man dies and goes to hell, where the Devil tells him he gets to choose his first punishment from a selection of **punishment chambers**.

First he shows him a room in which a young man is being whipped. The new arrival winces and asks to see the next room.

In this second room there is a middle-aged man being **tortured with fire**. The new man shudders and asks to see the third room.

The Devil opens the door to reveal an old man chained to the wall and getting a blow job from a **stunning blonde**. The newcomer immediately says he'll take this one.

The Devil leads the way into the room, taps the blonde on the shoulder and says, 'You can stop now. You've been relieved.'

PLAYGROUND ADVICE

Little Andy notices that his schoolfriend has a new watch. 'Where did you get that?' he asks him.

His friend explains that he heard the **bedsprings** creaking in his mum and dad's bedroom one night and ran in to see what was going on. He adds, 'My dad gave me a watch **to get rid of me**.'

Little Andy thinks this sounds like an easy way to get a present and so that night he listens out for the **creak of bedsprings**, then runs into his parents' bedroom.

'What do YOU want?' Andy's dad shouts.

'I want a watch,' says Andy.

'Well, then, sit down and shut up!' his dad answers.

Titillating Travel
&
Time Off Jokes

WHAT A VIEW

On the first day of her holiday, Samantha sunbathes on the roof of her hotel, **wearing a bikini**.

The next day, however, the rather buxom young lady decides to be true to her naturist side and strips off for a more even tan.

But she's barely settled herself when she hears **someone running** up the stairs. As she's lying on her stomach, she covers her bum with a towel.

'Excuse me, miss,' stammered the flustered assistant manager. 'The hotel is quite happy for guests to **sunbathe on the roof** but we would really appreciate you wearing a bikini as you did yesterday.'

'It shouldn't make any difference,' Samantha replies. 'It's not as if anybody can see me up here, and besides, I'm covered with a **towel**.'

'Not exactly; you're lying on the dining room skylight.'

IN THE DESERT

Two guys are stranded in the desert with nothing to eat or drink. Suddenly they spot a little hut and run up to it, half fearing it is **just a mirage**.

Yet when they knock on the door, an ugly, big, fat, smelly woman answers. The first man tells the lady about their plight and begs her for a drink.

The woman says, 'I'll give you a drink on **one condition** – you have to fuck me.'

The first man replies, 'I'd rather die of thirst than fuck you.'

The second man wants to live and so agrees to do the deed. He and the woman enter the hut, leaving the first man outside.

The woman says, 'Fuck me, then!'

The man says he will do it but only if she closes her eyes. He looks around the hut and sees a load of **corn on the cob** on a table. He picks one up, fucks her with it and chucks it out of the window. The woman groans with pleasure and asks for it again. The man agrees and repeats the act.

The woman is so satisfied that she says she will give both the man and his friend something to drink. The man calls his friend in and tells him that the woman is going to give both of them some water.

The friend replies, '**Fuck the water** – I want some more of that buttered corn.'

VENTRILOQUIST'S DUMMY

As part of a tour a ventriloquist stops to entertain in a small town club.

He's doing his usual routine – off-colour gags and '**dumb blonde**' jokes – when suddenly a smartly-dressed blonde stands up and says, 'I'm so tired of hearing these ridiculous blonde jokes! What gives you the right to stereotype women that way? How can the colour of a person's hair have any bearing on their fundamental worth as a human being?

It is idiots like you that prevent women like myself from being **respected at work** and in our communities and from reaching our full potential... because you and your anachronistic kind continue to perpetuate negative images against not only blondes, but women in general, for the sake of **cheap laughs**. You are a pathetic relic of the past, and what you do is not only contrary to discrimination laws in every civilised country, it is deeply offensive to people with modern sensibilities and basic respect for their fellow citizens. You should hang your head in shame, you pusillanimous little maggot.'

Embarrassed, the ventriloquist starts apologising, when suddenly **the blonde yells**, 'You stay out of this, mister! I'm talking to that little bastard on your knee!'

DRINK DRIVING

A man is driving along, minding his own business, when he's pulled over by the **police**.

The policeman walks up to the car and asks if he has been **drinking**.

Worried that he might have been weaving across the road, the man asks, 'Why? Was I driving badly?'

'No, you were driving very well,' replies the policeman. 'The ugly, **fat bird** in the passenger seat gave it away.'

REVENGE ON THE TAXI DRIVER

A businessman flies to Las Vegas and spends the weekend gambling. Unfortunately he doesn't have much success and ends up with just spare change and his return ticket. He knows he can get home if he can just get to the airport, so he goes to the front of the **casino**, hops into a taxi and explains his situation to the driver. He offers him his credit card numbers, his driver's license number, his home and business addresses and promises to **send money** once he gets home, but the driver is adamant that he doesn't give free rides and kicks the man out of his taxi.

The businessman hitchhikes to the airport and just manages to catch his flight.

The following year, the businessman returns to Las Vegas, having worked hard to regain his financial success. This time he wins a lot of money and is feeling really good about himself when he goes to get a taxi back to the airport. To his surprise, he spots the driver from the year before at the end of the line of taxis and decides to make him pay for refusing to help him.

He gets into the first taxi in line, and asks how much a ride to the airport costs. '**Fifteen bucks**,' the driver replies.

Then the businessman asks, 'And how much would you charge for a blow job on the way?'

'What? Who the hell do you think you are? Get the fuck out of my car!' the driver yells.

The businessman gets into each taxi in the line, and asks the same questions, getting the same **angry reply** each time. Then he gets into the last taxi and asks, 'How much for a ride to the airport?'

Not recognising him, the driver replies, 'Fifteen bucks.'

The businessman agrees and off they go. As they drive past the long line of taxis, the businessman gives a **big smile** and thumbs up sign to each driver.

What is soft and warm when you
go to bed, but hard and stiff
when you wake up?

Vomit.

SWALLOWING IT WHALE

A male and a female whale are swimming by the coast when the male suddenly spots the whaling ship that **killed his father** several years before.

Anxious to avenge his father's death, he concocts a plan to sink the ship and teach them a lesson. The female whale agrees to help him, and together they swim under the ship, blow air through their **blow holes** and knock the ship over.

But then the male whale notices that, although the ship has sunk, most of the **sailors** are making their way back to the shore either by swimming or in lifeboats. Not willing to let them escape, the male whale yells, 'They're going to shore – let's go gobble them up.'

'No way,' says the female whale. 'I said yes to the blow job, but I'm *not* swallowing seamen!'

STOP TAILGATING

A girl buys some underwear and explains to the sales assistant that she'd like to have something **embroidered** on her new **pants and bra**. The sales assistant tells her that would be fine and asks what she'd like.

'I'd like this sentence: "If you can read this you're too damn close",' replies the girl.

'Would you prefer **block or script letters?**'

'Braille,' she replies.

HOT CHILLI

A man goes into a pub and orders a pint and a bowl of hot chilli. 'I'm afraid the gent next to you got the last bowl,' the waitress explains.

So he settles for **just a pint**. When he sees that the man next to him has finished eating, but that the chilli bowl is still full, he asks,

'Are you going to eat that?'

The other man says, 'No. **You can have it**.'

The first man takes the bowl and is enjoying the **chilli** until he's eaten about half the bowlful and sees a dead mouse. He's so sickened that he pukes the chilli back into the bowl.

The other guy commiserates, 'That's about as far as I got too.'

GETTING WEIGHED

Joe and Rose are set up by their friends and on their first date, they decide to go to the fair. When they get there, **Joe asks Rose** what she wants to do first and she replies, 'Get weighed.' So Joe takes her to the man with the scales who guesses people's weight.

He looks at Rose and guesses wrongly that Rose weighs eight stone and eight pounds, so Rose collects a prize. Next they go on the **roller-coaster** and when that's finished Joe asks Rose what she wants to do. 'Get weighed,' she says. So they go back to the man with the scales, who guesses Rose's weight correctly this time, and the two go on the merry-go-round without collecting a prize. After that ride is over, Joe again asks Rose what she'd like to do. 'I want to get weighed!' she repeats.

Thinking Rose is a bit strange, Joe **makes an excuse** and ends the date, dropping her at her door with a peck on the cheek.

Inside Rose's friend is waiting to hear all the **gossip** and asks how the evening went.

'Wousy!' Rose sighs.

What's the difference between a Porsche and a hedgehog?

A hedgehog has pricks on the outside.

WELL ENDOWED

John and Fred have been friends for years and they often get together to chat about old times over a few pints. One night after **a couple of beers**, they both need to use the facilities at the same time. Although they are deep in conversation, Fred can't help noticing the size of John's manhood and is more than a **little envious**. 'I say, old chap, that's a rather large trouser snake you've got there.'

'Yes, it is, isn't it?' agrees John. 'Although it wasn't always like this. Got it done over on **Harley Street**. Cost me a grand but I think it's worth it.'

Fred was so impressed that he booked an appointment and headed off to Harley Street the next morning.

Six months later, when he met John again, he was eager to tell him the good news and also wanted to **boast** how he'd got his done for a much better price.

'Five hundred pounds? I don't believe it. I went to the same doctor at the same address. How did you get it done for less?' John complained. 'You'll have to let me **take a look**, old boy.' So they went to the gents where John had a look at Fred and burst out laughing. 'Ah, Fred. They gave you my old one.'

007'S WATCH

007 walks into a bar and takes a seat next to a very **beautiful woman**. He gives her a long, admiring look and then casually glances at his watch. The woman notices this and asks, 'Is your date running late?'

'No,' he replies suavely. 'I was just testing my new **state-of-the-art** watch. It's Q's latest invention.'

The intrigued woman gushes, 'A state-of-the-art watch? What's so special about it?'

'It tells me all about the person sitting next to me, by using **alpha waves** to telepathically talk to me,' he explains.

'What's it telling you now?'

'Well, it says you're not wearing any panties...'

The woman **giggles**. 'Well, it's not working properly because I am wearing panties!'

007 shakes his head, taps his watch and sighs, 'Must be an hour fast!'

MOTHERFUCKER

After a great round of golf, three friends are having a **celebratory drink** in the clubhouse when another man approaches them and, pointing to one of them, announces, 'I've fucked your mum!'

The man resumes drinking at the bar, leaving the three friends **looking confused**.

After a while, he walks back to them and shouts, 'Your mum sucked my cock!' At this stage the three friends are tired of his **outbursts** and fifteen minutes later, when the man declares, 'I've had your mum up the arse!' one young man springs to his feet and yells, 'Go home, Dad, I think you've had enough.'

THE SHY GUY AND THE STUDENT

A young man has been sitting in a bar for an hour, trying to work up the courage to approach the **gorgeous young lady** sitting at another table. Finally he approaches her and asks if she would mind if he sat with her for a while.

'Of course I won't go to bed with you!' she screams at him. Completely **embarrassed** and aware that everybody is looking at him, he rushes back to his table with his eyes glued to the floor.

The woman walks over a little while later and smiles. 'I'm **sorry** that I embarrassed you. It's part of an assignment for my psychology course – I have to examine how **people react** in embarrassing situations.'

The young man looks at her and then yells, 'You've got to be joking – two hundred quid?'

THE MUSICAL OCTOPUS

A man walks into a bar and announces, 'This is my pet octopus and I bet fifty quid that **he can play** whatever musical instrument you give to him.'

Several people agree to take the bet and one hands over his guitar. The octopus picks it up, tunes the strings and plays the guitar like a rock star. **Shaking his head** the guitar's owner hands over the fifty pounds.

Convinced he's going to win the money, another man gives the octopus a trumpet. The octopus takes the instrument, loosens up the keys, and plays a cool jazz solo. The octopus's owner pockets another **fifty quid**.

A few moments later the owner of the bar hands the octopus a set of **bagpipes** and promises the owner one hundred pounds if the octopus can play them.

The octopus looks at the bagpipes, picks them up, then turns them over, and **looks at them** from another angle.

His owner is a bit confused so he goes up to the octopus and tells him to **stop messing around** and play the set of bagpipes instead of looking at it.

'What do you mean play it?' asks the octopus. 'If I can figure out how to get it out of its pyjamas I'm gonna fuck it!'

What's the worst thing about being a test-tube baby?

You know your dad's a wanker.

THE MAN, THE OSTRICH AND THE CAT

A man walks into a pub with an ostrich and a cat. 'What can I get you?' asks the bemused barman.

The man replies, 'Make mine a pint,' and, turning to the ostrich asks, 'What do you want?' 'I'll have the same,' replies the ostrich. The man asks the cat what he's drinking, and the cat replies, 'I'll have a half, but I ain't fuckin' paying.'

The barman gives them their drinks and says, 'That'll be £6.10, please.'

The **man digs around** for the money in his pocket and, to the barman's surprise, lays exactly £6.10 in loose change on the bar.

Some time later the man, the ostrich and the small cat come back to the bar. 'Make mine **another pint**,' says the man. 'Same here,' says the ostrich. 'I'll have a half, but I ain't fuckin' paying,' says the cat.

'That'll be £6.10,' says the barman. Again the man digs around for the money in his pocket and lays exactly £6.10 in loose change on the bar.

This happens a couple more times, and the barman is **quite baffled**. Finally he calls last orders and the man, the ostrich and the cat come back to the bar.

'As it's last orders,' says the man, 'I'm going to have a large scotch,' and he asks the ostrich and the cat what they want. 'Make mine a **large scotch** too,' the ostrich says. 'Just a small scotch for me, but I ain't fuckin' paying,' the cat says.

The barman hands them their drinks and grins mischievously as he says, 'That'll be £6.90, please.' Yet unbelievably the man digs around for the money in his pocket and lays exactly £6.90 in loose change on the bar.

When the barman calls **closing time**, the unusual threesome drink up and turn to leave, but the barman can contain his curiosity no longer. 'Before you go I have to ask you something. How come when it's time to pay you always manage to come up with exactly the right change from your pocket, every time?'

'Well,' says the man, 'a few years ago I helped an old lady and when she died she left me her house. It was just a rambling, pretty rundown place, but when I was clearing out the attic I found an old lamp, and when I rubbed it to clean it up this genie appeared and gave me **two wishes**.'

'That's amazing,' says the barman. 'What did you wish for?'

'First of all,' says the man, 'I wished that whenever I ever need to pay for anything I just put my hand in my pocket and the right money will always be there.'

'Genius,' says the barman. 'Much better than just wishing for a **million pounds**. This way you will always be as rich as you want.'

'Oh, yes,' agrees the man. 'It's the best thing I ever did. If I want to buy a pint the money will always be there. And the same goes for anything else – if I want to buy a **Mercedes Benz** I know the exact money I need will be there.'

The man starts to make his way out of the pub, but the barman still has one last question. 'Your **drinking companions** – we don't get many ostriches or cats drinking in here.'

The man's expression turns to one of melancholy as he explains, 'That was the **worst thing** I ever did. You see, on my second wish I asked for a bird with long legs and a tight pussy.'

ANY PAPER?

A young man goes into a pub and spots a beautiful woman in the corner. After a few drinks they've really hit it off and decide to **go to her place**.

As they go into the living room, she whispers, 'You'll have to be really quiet because my parents are asleep upstairs and they'll kill you if they catch you.'

They settle down on the sofa and things are getting steamy when the man feels the alcohol begin to take effect on his **bladder**.

'You'll have to use the kitchen sink,' she tells him. 'The bathroom is next to my parents' bedroom.'

A little dubious but needing to go badly, the young man goes to the **kitchen** to do his business. A few minutes later, he pops his head round the door and asks, 'Do you have any paper?'

JACK THE SPERM

Once there was a sperm named Jack. While all the other sperm were **lazily swimming** around, Jack was stretching, doing sprints and lifting weights.

One day all the other sperm asked him, 'Why don't you just **take it easy** like us?'

Jack replied, 'When the time comes, I'm making sure I'm the first one there.'

Finally it was time. All the **sperm were swimming** along with Jack leading the way.

Suddenly he stopped dead in his tracks, turned around and headed back.

'Why are you going back?' the others asked.

He called out, 'Back up boys, it's a BLOW JOB!'

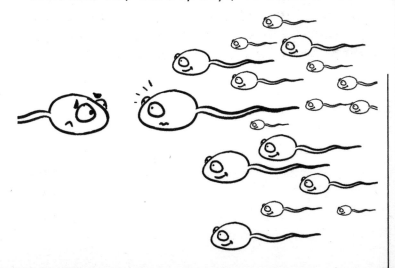

NUN TRICK

A businessman gets on a bus and sits next to a nun in the front seat. He leans over to her and asks if she would have **sex with him**.

Shocked, the nun politely refuses and gets off at the next stop.

As the bus gets going again, the driver says to the businessman, 'I know a way you can get that nun to have sex with you.'

The businessman begs him to explain how, so the bus driver tells him that every Wednesday evening **at midnight** the nun goes to the church graveyard to pray to the Lord. 'If you went dressed in long flowing robes and covered in glowing powder,' says the bus driver, 'you could say you were God and command her to have sex with you.'

So that Wednesday, the businessman goes to the graveyard and waits for the nun. Right on schedule, the nun shows up. Once she begins her prayers, the businessman comes out from his **hiding place**, dressed up to look like the Lord in all His glowing glory. 'I am the Lord. I have heard your prayers and I will answer them, but first I command you to have sex with me,' he says.

The nun assents but asks for anal sex so she might **preserve her virginity**. The businessman agrees and immediately has sex with the nun.

Once he's finished, he rips off his mask and cries, 'Ha ha – I'm the businessman!'

The nun, in turn, rips off her mask and shouts, 'Ha ha – I'm the bus driver!'

SHIPWRECKED

A young man is taking the trip of a lifetime on a cruise ship. Then, on only the fourth day of the cruise, the ship hits some rocks and sinks. Thankfully the young man, Dave, manages to grab on to a piece of driftwood and swims a few miles through the **shark-infested waters** to a desert island. Exhausted, he flops down on the beach and tries to recover his breath.

With his strength slowly returning, he turns his head and notices a **young woman** lying near him, unconscious. She is the only other survivor from the sinking ship. Dave crawls over to her, gives her mouth-to-mouth resuscitation and manages to get her breathing again.

She gazes up at him and says, 'You saved my life – **you're my hero.**' Suddenly he realises that the woman is Pamela Anderson.

Days and weeks go by. Pamela and Dave have made the island their home. They've built a hut, they eat tropical fruit fresh from the trees, and they feel that they've found paradise. Pamela, still grateful to her knight in shining armour, is madly in love with Dave, and they're **making passionate love** morning, noon and night.

Then one day she notices that he doesn't look too happy. 'What's the matter, my darling?'

she asks, 'Our life here is perfect. Is there something wrong? Can I do anything to lift your spirits?'

He says, 'Well, Pam, maybe there is. Would you mind putting on my shirt?'

'Sure,' she says. He takes off his shirt and she puts it on.

'And now my trousers?' he asks. Pamela is willing to do anything to make him feel better so she puts them on.

'OK, now could you put my hat on and draw a **moustache** above your lip?' he asks.

'Anything for you, sweetie,' she says.

Finally he asks her to start walking along the beach around the island, which she does. **Dave sets off** in the other direction.

They meet up halfway around the island a little while later. He rushes up to her, grabs her by the shoulders, and says, 'Mate! You'll never believe who I'm shagging!'

BY THE SEASIDE

Cheryl is sitting on a bench in a quiet park next to a good-looking man reading a book. 'Hi there,' she says, '**Do you like films?**'

'Yes, I do,' he answers, then returns to his book.

Cheryl tries to keep the conversation going. 'Do you like swimming?'

The man looks up from his book again politely. 'Yes, I do,' he says before getting back to his reading.

Not one to be put off, Cheryl asks, 'Do you like pussycats?'

With that, the man throws his book to the ground and **pounces on Cheryl**, ravaging her in a way she's never known. As the man picks up his book, Cheryl pulls herself to a sitting position and pants, 'How did you know that was what I wanted?'

The man replies, 'How did you know my name was Katz?'

BARBIE AND GI JOE

A little girl is queuing to see Father Christmas. Finally it's her turn to climb up on **Father Christmas's** lap.

He asks, 'What would you like me to bring you for Christmas?'

The little girl replies, 'I want a Barbie and GI Joe.'

Father Christmas looks at the little girl, **puzzled**, and says, 'I thought Barbie comes with Ken.'

'No,' **says the little girl**. 'She comes with GI Joe; she fakes it with Ken.'

BIRTHDAY GIFT

A man has been seeing a **lovely woman** for a short while and needs to buy a present for her birthday. It needs to be personal but not too personal and after a lot of thinking he decides that a pair of **gloves** will be perfect for her.

He goes to the shop and, with the help of her sister, chooses a pair of white gloves. At the same time the sister buys a pair of **panties** for herself. Without realising, the sales assistant mixes the items up and gives the sister the package with the gloves and hands the man the panties.

The man sends his package to his girlfriend with the **following note:**

I bought these because I noticed you do not wear any in the evening. I wanted to buy the long ones with the buttons, but instead chose ones like your sister wears as they are easier to remove.

These are a delicate shade, but the sales assistant who helped me has a pair that she has been wearing for the past three weeks and they are hardly soiled at all. I had her try yours on for me and she looked very smart.

I wish I was there to put them on for you the first time, as no doubt other hands will come into contact with them before I have a chance to see you again.

When you take them off, remember to blow in them before putting them away as they will naturally be a little damp from wearing.

Just think how many times I will kiss them during the coming year. I hope you will wear them for me Friday night.

All my love.

P.S. The latest style is to wear them folded down with a little fur showing.

What's the difference between a tampon and a cowboy hat?

A cowboy hat is for an arsehole.

SEX IN THE JUNGLE

When Jane first met Tarzan in the jungle, she was immediately attracted to him. She asked him lots of questions about his life, including how he managed for sex.

'What's sex?' he asked.

She explained it to him and he said, 'Tarzan use **hole in trunk of tree**.'

Alarmed, she said, 'No, no, Tarzan – that's all wrong. I will show you how to do it properly.' She took her clothes off, lay down on the ground and **spread her legs** wide open. 'Here,' she said, pointing. 'This is where it goes.'

Tarzan ripped off his loincloth, **stepped closer** and then kicked her in the crotch with all his might. Jane could **hardly breathe** in her agony. Finally she managed to gasp, 'Why on earth did you do that?'

'Tarzan check for bees!'

THE RABBIT AND THE BEAR

A bear is chasing a rabbit in a forest when suddenly a frog appears in front of them and tells them that he is a visitor from a **magical forest**. He adds that he is upset that they aren't living in peace and promises each of them three wishes if they agree to stop chasing each other.

The bear immediately wishes that all the other bears in the forest **were female**. And just like that, the other bears are female. But the rabbit wishes for a crash helmet. The bear thinks really hard before making his second wish and this time he wishes that all the other bears in the country were female. Again **his wish is granted** and the rest of the bears become female. The rabbit wishes for a motorcycle.

The bear laughs to himself, thinking, 'That rabbit is so stupid, he's making such ridiculous wishes.' For his final wish, the bear takes his time deciding what it is that he really wants. He wants to make this one count and eventually he wishes… that all the other bears in the world were female. And poof, all the other bears are female. The rabbit **puts on his helmet** and jumps on his bike. 'For my final wish,' he smiles, looking at the bear, 'I wish that the bear was gay.'

THREE IN A BED

Three guys spend the night at a hotel but because they're broke, they can only afford one room and end up sharing a **double bed**.

When they wake in the morning, the guy on the right says, 'I had a fantastic dream last night – this gorgeous girl **gave me a hand job**.'

A little surprised, the guy on the left says, 'That's so strange. I did too.'

'Lucky for you guys,' yawns the **guy in the middle**. 'I just dreamt I was skiing.'

TOO FAR GONE

A young man with an adventurous girlfriend is showing off his new sports car. Thrilled at the speed, she agrees to **take off her clothes** if he can manage 200 mph and sure enough, when the speedometer reads 200 mph, she strips.

Distracted, the man loses control of the car. It skids onto gravel and flips over. **The naked girl** is thrown clear, but the young man is trapped beneath the steering wheel.

The girl is faced with a dilemma: she has to find help for her boyfriend but she's naked and her clothes have disappeared. 'Take my shoe and cover yourself. **Just get help**,' begs the young man. 'There's a petrol station down the road.'

Holding the shoe over her privates, the girl runs down the road to the petrol station, dashes inside, still covering herself with the shoe, and finds the proprietor. '**My boyfriend's stuck!** You have to help me.' He looks at her and then, shaking his head, says, 'Sorry, there's nothing I can do... he's in too far.'

PISS POOR AIM

At his local one night Dave asks the landlord, 'Rob, you place a bet or two from time to time, don't you?'

'Every now and then. Why do you want to know?'

'I bet you a **hundred quid** that I can piss into a shot glass at the end of your bar without spilling a drop.'

Thinking that Dave must be the biggest idiot in town, and that he could do with an easy hundred quid, Rob agrees to **take the bet**. Rob strolls down to the other end of the bar

and positions a shot glass on the end. He walks back behind the bar and says, 'Right, then, show us what you've got.'

Dave **unzips his fly** and starts pissing all over the place: over the bar counter, the walls, the bottles of booze, and all over Rob.

Rob doubles up with laughter and almost falls over. Then he sees that Dave is standing at the bar grinning. 'You've got **nothing to smile about**, you just lost a hundred pounds,' Rob says.

'Well, actually, you see the man over there, the one in the big hat writing out a cheque?'

'Yeah, I see him.'

'About an hour ago I bet him a grand that I could **piss all over your bar**, your booze, your walls and you, and not only would you not be mad, you would laugh hysterically about it.'

LATE HOME

While out drinking one night, a man turns to his friend and says, 'I always try to be considerate when I come home after **a night drinking**. I make sure I turn off the headlights before I get near the driveway, then I turn off the engine and coast into the garage. I take my shoes off outside the front door. I undress in the bathroom and I'm always really quiet when I **sneak into bed** but my wife still wakes up and screams at me for coming home so late.'

'Well,' says his friend, 'you're doing **it all wrong**. You should do what I do. I screech into the driveway, slam the front door, stomp up the stairs, fling my shoes into the wardrobe, jump into bed, slap my wife's arse and say, "How about a blow job?" And she's always sound asleep.'

BUS STOP

A beautiful young woman in a tight mini skirt is waiting at a busy bus stop. When it's her turn to get on, she realises that her **skirt is too tight** and she can't get her leg on to the first step of the bus.

Embarrassed, she smiles at the bus driver and reaches behind to unzip her skirt a little and get enough slack to raise her leg. But she still can't make the step. She reaches behind herself again to unzip her skirt a little more but, to her dismay, she just cannot **raise her leg**. When, after a third effort, she still can't step onto the bus, the large man standing behind her picks her up and places her gently in front of the driver.

She's furious that he **dared to touch her** without her permission and vents her frustration at him, screaming, 'I don't even know who you are!'

The man smiles and replies, 'Usually I'd agree with you, but after you unzipped my fly three times, I decided we were friends.'

Why do they call it the Wonderbra®?

✦ ✦ ✦

Because when you take it off you wonder where her tits went.

A GOOD DENTIST

A man and woman meet in a pub and get along so well that they decide to go back to the woman's flat. A few drinks later, the man **takes his socks off** and then washes his hands. Next, he unbuttons his shirt and washes his hands again. The woman says to him, 'You must be a dentist.'

The man is surprised as she has guessed his profession correctly. 'How did you work that out?'

'It's obvious,' she answers. 'You keep washing your hands.'

Before long, **they are in bed** and making love. Afterwards the woman says, 'You must be a really good dentist.'

The man is clearly flattered and says, 'Actually, yes, I am a **good dentist**. How did you work that out?'

'I didn't feel a thing!'

JELLY BABY'S NASTY RASH

Jelly Baby has developed a nasty rash down below so he decides to go and see a doctor to get an **expert opinion**.

The jelly doctor examines him and then looks at Jelly Baby and says, 'I'm not sure what's wrong, Jelly Baby. We'll have to take a **jelly sample,** and then you must come back in two days.'

So Jelly Baby goes back a couple of days later for the test result and the doctor says, 'We've got the result and I'm **very sorry**, Jelly Baby – you've picked up a sexually transmitted disease.'

Jelly Baby looks at the doctor and says, 'Well, is that it?'

'You don't sound very **surprised**,' says the doctor.

Jelly Baby replies, 'I'm not – I've been sleeping with Allsorts.'

What's the difference between snowmen and snowwomen?

Snowballs.

HARD OF HEARING

An old man visits the health clinic and tells his doctor he thinks his wife may be hard of hearing. 'How can I check?' he asks.

The doctor replies, 'If you don't want to **ask her outright**, you could try this: say something to her when you get home. If she doesn't respond, then move a bit closer and repeat what you said. Keep doing this until she does hear and you will be able to tell **how deaf she is**.'

The old man thanks the doctor for this advice and sets off home. As he opens the front door he looks along the hallway and sees his wife in the kitchen, with her back to him.

He closes the door quietly and says to his wife, 'Hello love, **I'm home**. What's for dinner?' There is no answer, so he moves down the hallway a little and says again, 'Hello love, I'm home. What's for dinner?' Again, he gets no response, so he walks into the kitchen and says, 'Hello love, I'm home. What's for dinner?' Still she doesn't reply, so he stands right beside her, **lightly touches her** arm and says, 'Hello love, I'm home. What's for dinner?'

With that she reels around and shouts at him, 'Toad in the hole, for the fourth fucking time, you deaf bastard!'

THE MUTE'S
IDEAL WOMAN

Two men walk into a bar. Bill has no voice and relies on his friend **John to speak** for him. The other men in the bar are curious to know what kind of woman he likes, so Bill points to his head and John tells them, 'He wants an intelligent woman.' When he **rubs his palm** with his thumb, John explains, 'He wants a woman with money.' Bill then opens his hands, bends his fingers and **bounces** them by his chest.

Bemused, John asks, 'Why on earth do you want a woman with arthritis?'

THE CHECK-UP

An elderly couple arrange to have their annual medical examination the same day. First to be examined is the old man. The doctor gives him a clean **bill of health** and then asks, 'Do you have any medical complaints that you would like to discuss with me?'

'Actually, yes,' says the man. 'At first, after I have sex with my wife I am hot and sweaty. And then, the second time we have sex I feel quite chilly.'

The doctor **scratches his chin**. 'This is very interesting,' he says. 'I will do some research and get back to you.'

Next he examines the old lady and tells her, 'You appear to be in good health. Do you have any medical complaints that you would like to discuss with me?' The old lady says that she has no questions or concerns.

The doctor then says, 'Your husband had an **unusual concern**. He told me that he is hot and sweaty after the first time he has sex with you and then quite chilly after the second time. Do you know why?'

'Oh, that old fool!' she replies. 'That's because the first time is in July and the second time is in December!'

SEX PROBLEM

A doctor sees a patient who tells him, 'I've got this sex problem, doc.'

'I see,' says the doctor. 'Describe for me your average day.'

The man replies, 'Well, it all starts in the middle of the night. My wife wakes me without fail at about three in the morning for **a roll in the sack** and then again at about five o'clock so we can make love for a couple of hours before I go to work.'

'Right, I see,' says the doctor.

'No, that's not all,' the man says. 'I take the train to work and every day I meet this girl and we get a compartment to ourselves and **have sex** for the whole journey.'

'Right, now I see,' the doctor says.

'No, wait,' the man tells him. 'At work my secretary really **fancies me** and I have to give her one in the stationery cupboard.'

'Right, now I see,' says the doctor.

'No, you don't,' the man says. 'At lunch I go along to the canteen where I see this dinner lady I'm very fond of and we **sneak out the back** for a bit of how's your father.'

'Now I understand,' says the doctor.

'No, wait,' the man interrupts. 'Back at work in the afternoon, my boss, a very demanding lady, says she must **have me** and if I refuse she'll give me the sack.'

'Ahh,' says the doctor, 'now I get it.'

'No, there's more,' the man continues. 'When I get home my wife is **so happy to see me** she gives me a blow job before dinner and then we have sex afterwards.'

'So what's the problem?' the doctor finally asks.

'Well,' says the man, 'it hurts when I masturbate.'

Do you know why hippos do their romancing underwater?

It's the only way to keep a five-hundred-pound pussy wet.

PATIENT GETS THE BLUES

One morning a man arrives at the doctor's surgery in a bit of a state because one of his testicles has turned blue.

The doctor tells the man to undress then he examines him briefly and determines that he must have his testicle removed at once.

'You **must be mad**! Why would I let you do that?' screams the unfortunate patient.

The doctor looks at him and asks rhetorically, 'Do you want to die?' and the patient agrees to have his testicle removed.

Two weeks later he's back in the surgery. 'Doc, I don't know what to do – my other ball is blue now.'

The doctor's diagnosis is the same: the patient must have his testicle removed to **save his life**.

Understandably, the man is not too keen to go ahead with the operation but agrees reluctantly.

Another two weeks go by and the man is again in a panic. 'My penis has turned blue now. You have to help me. What's wrong with me?'

The doctor briefly examines the man again and concludes that, this time, the man's penis must go. The man is desperate to **avoid the operation**. 'How will I pee?' he asks feebly.

'That won't be a problem – we'll insert an plastic pipe and that'll take care of that.'

The man tearfully agrees and his penis is removed. A few weeks after the penis removal he storms into the surgery, yelling that the plastic pipe is now blue. The doctor is **shocked**. 'What?'

'What the hell is going on, doc?'

After a more detailed examination the doctor looks at his patient and says, 'Hmm, I think it's the jeans.'

TWO FEMALE CYCLISTS

Two young women are riding their old bikes down the back streets of **Amsterdam** late one evening.

As it gets **darker**, the women become increasingly nervous. One turns to her friend and says, 'You know, I've **never come** this way before.'

The other woman says, 'I know, I think it's the cobblestones.'

THE FREE BEER

The new bloke in town walks into a pub and reads a sign that hangs over the bar:

FREE BEER FOR THE PERSON
WHO CAN PASS THE TEST!

Never one to say no to free beer, he asks the bartender what the test is.

'You see that gallon of pepper tequila over there?' the barman says. 'First you have to drink the whole gallon all at once, and without **making a face**. Second, there's an alligator out back with a sore tooth and you have to remove it with your bare hands. And third, you have to make things right for the woman upstairs who's never had an orgasm.'

'As much as I would love the free beer, I won't do it,' the man insists. 'You would have to be crazy to drink a gallon of **pepper tequila**, never mind any of the other requirements!'

After a few hours and more than a few drinks, the man suddenly demands, 'Wherez zat teeqeelah?' A tad unsteadily he grabs the gallon of tequila with both hands, and downs it with a **big slurp** and tears streaming down his face. Then he staggers out back and soon all the people in the pub hear an awful **screaming** and pounding and then silence. The man stumbles back into the bar with his shirt ripped and big scratches covering his body.

'Now,' he slurs, 'where's that woman with the sore tooth?'

Why do they call PMT PMT?

Because Mad Cow Disease was
already taken.

DOCTOR'S ORDERS

A woman takes her husband to see the doctor. After examining the man, the doctor sends him to the waiting room and asks to see his wife alone.

He tells her, 'Your husband is suffering from a very severe **stress disorder**. Unless you do the following, your husband is sure to die. Prepare a healthy breakfast for him every morning. Be pleasant at all times. Make him a **nutritious meal** for lunch. For dinner you should cook him something especially nice. Don't burden him with chores. Don't talk to him about your problems; it will only make his **stress worse**. Do not nag him. And, this is the most important part, make love with your husband several times a week. Do this for the next twelve months and I think your husband will regain his health completely.'

Driving home, the husband asks his wife, 'So, what did the **doctor say?**'

'He said you're going to die,' she replies.

KISS ME, DOCTOR

'Doctor, doctor, I want you to kiss me,' a patient says.

'No, I'm sorry, that oversteps the patient-doctor relationship boundary,' says the doctor.

Ten minutes later **the patient pleads**, 'Doctor, please, just one kiss.'

'No, I'm sorry, I really can't,' he says.

After another few minutes, she begs him, 'Please, *please* kiss me!'

'Look,' says the doctor, 'it's **out of the question**. In fact, I probably shouldn't even be fucking you.'

CURE FOR HEADACHES

After suffering from terrible headaches for several years – and trying all the cures he could find, without relief – a man is referred to the world's greatest **headache specialist**. When asked what his symptoms are, he replies, 'I get these awful headaches, which feel like a knife cutting through my scalp and…'

'And a dull **throbbing** behind your left ear?' interrupts the specialist.

'Yes! Oh, God, how did you know? That's it exactly!'

'Ah, well, I also experienced those blinding headaches, many years ago now. But I found a cure: every day for two weeks I gave my wife oral sex. Every time she came, she **squeezed her legs** together so tightly that the pressure relieved the tension in my head. Try that and come back to me in two weeks to let me know how it goes.'

The man comes back two weeks later, ecstatic that he hasn't had a headache since he started the treatment. 'Doctor, **I feel wonderful!** I'm a new man! My headaches are finally gone! I'm so grateful. And, by the way… great house.'

LAB TALK

There are three Labrador retrievers – brown, golden and black – sitting in the waiting room at the vet's and they strike up a conversation.

The black lab turns to the brown lab and says, 'So what are you doing here?'

The brown lab replies, 'I'm a pisser. **I piss on everything** – the armchair, the oven, the cat and the kids. But I went too far last night when I pissed on my owner's bed while he was sleeping in it.'

The black lab says, 'What do you think the vet's going to do?'

'Give me Prozac, I expect,' the brown lab replies. 'All the vets are prescribing it. It's the solution for everything.'

He then turns to the golden lab and asks, 'Why are you here?'

The golden lab says, 'I'm a digger. I dig up the garden, I dig up flowers and trees in the park, I dig just for the fun of it. Indoors I dig up the carpets. But it was the **final straw** last night when I dug a great big hole in my owner's settee.'

'So what are they going to do to you?' the black lab asks him.

'Reckon it'll be Prozac for me too,' the golden lab says. Then he turns to the black lab and asks, 'So what are you at the vet's office for?'

'I'm a humper,' the black lab says. 'I can't stop humping: the cat, a pillow, the table, legs – whatever. I see it, I have to **hump it**. Yesterday, after my owner had just had a shower, she bent down to dry between her toes and I just couldn't help myself. I hopped up on her back and started humping away.'

The golden and brown labs exchange a knowing look and say, 'So, **Prozac** for you too?'

The black lab says, 'No, I'm here to get my claws clipped.'

MAGIC SEX

A bloke approaches a girl in a pub and asks, 'How about a **game** of "Magic Sex"?'

She gives him a puzzled look and says, 'What's that?'

He explains, 'We go to **my house** and fuck, and then you disappear.'

HOW DO I LOOK?

A young woman, worried about her bed-wetting problem, visits her doctor for advice. He takes all her details, asks several questions and then tells her to go behind the screen and undress.

After that she should stand on her hands facing a full-length mirror. Although she's **a little shocked**, she decides to go ahead with the doctor's instructions as she's desperate for help with her problem. Once she is in position the doctor asks her to **open her legs** and then promptly rests his chin on her private parts. After muttering to himself for a few minutes, the doctor appears quite positive and tells the young woman that she can get dressed again.

Once she's dressed, he tells her that her problem is caused by **drinking too much** liquid before bedtime. Confused, the woman asks, 'What was the point of the exercise in front of the mirror? How did that help?'

He replies absent-mindedly, 'My wife is right, a beard would suit me.'

What's the definition of trust?

Two cannibals giving each
other a blow job.

HEAVENLY LIGHT

An elderly couple visit the doctor for their yearly physicals. The husband is the first to have his check-up. 'Well, Mr Johnson, you're **in great shape** for a man your age,' says the doctor.

The old man proudly replies, 'I should be. I don't smoke, I don't drink and the good Lord looks out for me.'

'What do you mean?' asks the doctor.

The elderly patient explains, 'Take last night. I got up in the middle of the night to **use the loo** and the good Lord turned the bathroom light on for me so I wouldn't fall over.'

'Right,' says the doctor, a little puzzled. 'Well, if you could please send your wife in now.'

The old man leaves and his wife comes in. After examining her, the doctor says, 'Mrs Johnson, you're in great shape for a woman your age.'

She smiles and replies, 'I should think so too. I don't smoke, I don't drink…'

The doctor interrupts her, 'And the **good Lord** looks after you, right? Your husband just told me the same thing.'

'What are you talking about?' asks the old woman, **confused**.

'Your husband was just saying how the good Lord looks out for him. Like last night when he got **out of bed** to use the toilet and the good Lord turned the bathroom light on for him.'

'Damn it!' the old woman snaps. 'I knew he was pissing in the fridge again.'

I CAN'T HEAR YOU

An old man with a hearing problem asks his wife to come along to his doctor's appointment. The doctor greets them both and then asks the man to remove his shirt.

The old man turns to his wife and yells, 'What?' His wife leans closer and shouts, 'Take your shirt off!' The old man nods and **takes his shirt off**.

The doctor then asks the old man to lean his head back so that he can look down his throat.

Again the old man shouts, 'What?' and his wife leans closer and yells, 'Tip your head back and **open your mouth**.' The old man nods and tips his head back.

'Right, now I need a urine sample, a stool sample and a semen sample,' says the doctor towards the end of the **examination**.

The old man yells, 'What?' and his wife gets closer and shouts, 'Give the doctor your underpants!'

MURPHY'S FIGHT

One night, Murphy limps into his local on crutches, with his face all bruised and with one arm in a sling. '**What the hell** happened to you, Murphy?' exclaims the barman.

'Ah sure, I had a bit of a **disagreement** with Mr Riley.'

'Mr Riley?' asks the barman in disbelief. 'You're bigger than him. He must have had something in his hand to be able to give you such a beating.'

'Indeed, he **had a shovel**,' Murphy explains.

'And didn't you have anything in your hand?'

'Aye, I was holding Mrs Riley's titties, and beautiful things they are too, but they're not much use in a fight.'

MIKE'S RED RING

Mike visits his doctor in a bit of a panic, after noticing a red rash around his **you-know-what**.

'Doctor,' he says, 'I've got this red ring around my thing. What is it and how do I get rid of it? If my girlfriend sees this, there's no saying what she'll do.'

The doctor examines him and then, shaking his head, writes a **prescription** for some pills. 'It's difficult to say what it is exactly but take these pills every day for the next week and if it hasn't cleared up, come back and see me again.'

But, even though Mike takes the pills, a week later the **red ring** is still there. Even more worried than before, he goes back to his doctor. Sighing, the doctor writes another prescription, for stronger medication this time, and gives Mike the same instructions as before: 'Take the capsules for a week and if there's no change, come back and see me.'

When Mike goes back to his doctor a week later, the red ring is still there. This time the doctor gives him a cream and tells him to **rub it onto** his manhood every day for a week and see what happens.

After a week, he pays the doctor a visit, thrilled that the red ring is gone and curious about the nature of the cream. 'Doc, that stuff was great! What was in the tube?'

'Lipstick remover.'

How do you annoy a female archaeologist?

Give her a used tampon and ask her what period it comes from.

IF YOU WANT A JOB DOING...

Ben has been asking Lisa to go out with him for ages and finally she agrees. He takes her to a swish restaurant, buys her the most **expensive meal** on the menu and they share a bottle of the finest wine.

Driving her home, he pulls into Lovers' Lane and stops the car. They start kissing and he begins to feel **very aroused**, so he puts his hand under her skirt. Lisa stops him, telling him she's a virgin and that's the way she wants to stay. 'OK,' he says, 'just give me a blow job, then.'

'No way!' she says. 'I'm not having that thing anywhere **near my mouth!**'

So he says, 'All right, just a hand job.'

'How do I do that?' she asks.

'Well,' Ben answers, 'remember when you were little and you used to shake up a Coke bottle and **spray it all over your brother?**' She nods. 'It's just like that.'

She agrees to do it and gets on with the job in hand. A few moments later, he **screams** out in pain, snot running out of his nose and wax bursting out of his ears. 'What's wrong?' Lisa cries.

'TAKE YOUR BLOODY THUMB OFF THE END!'

DENTAL TREATMENT

Carol has been having a passionate after-hours affair with her **gorgeous** new dentist when one day he declares miserably that the affair has to end. 'Carol, darling, isn't your husband **suspicious?**'

'Of course he isn't,' she assures her lover. 'If he's so stupid that he still hasn't realised that we've been seeing each other these last six months, he's never going to work it out.'

'**Good point**,' he agrees. 'But you've only got one tooth left!'

THREE WOMEN
AT THE BAR

Three women are drinking at the bar.

The first one says, '**My hole's so big**, my boyfriend can shove his whole fist up it.'

'That's nothing,' the second woman says. 'Mine's so big my hubby can fit his entire head up it.'

The third woman **laughs** so hard she falls down the stool.

LIFELONG VIRGIN

In a tiny village there once lived an old maid. Despite her old age, she was still a virgin and very **proud of it**. She knew she wasn't long for this earth, so she told the local **undertaker** what inscription she wanted on her gravestone:

'Born a virgin, lived a virgin, died a virgin.'

Only a few days later, the old maid died peacefully, and the undertaker told his men what they were to put on her **gravestone**. Now these men were lazy good-for-nothings and decided the inscription was too long. They simply wrote:

'Returned unopened.'

WHO LIKES IT MORE?

A man and a woman are drinking in a bar when they get into an argument about which gender **enjoys sex** more.

The man says, 'It's obvious that men enjoy sex more than women do. That's why we're so **obsessed** with getting laid.'

'That doesn't prove anything,' the woman retorts. 'Think about this. When you have an **itchy ear** and you put your little finger in it and wiggle it about for a bit, then **pull it out**, which feels better – your ear or your finger?'

WIND-TASTIC JOKES

Minge-tastic Marriage Jokes

OLD AGE SEX

A young man is engaged to be married and asks his **grandfather** about sex. In particular, he wants to know how often a couple should have it.

His grandfather says, 'At first, you want it all the time and get between the sheets several times a day. After a while, the urge wears off and you only have sex about **once a week**. Then, as time goes by, this turns into once a month. When you hit old age, you might have it once a year, if you're lucky.'

The young man asks, 'What about you and Grandma now?'

His grandfather replies, 'Oh, we just have **oral sex now**.'

'Really?' the young man asks, surprised.

'Yes,' his grandfather answers. 'She goes to her bedroom and I go to mine. She yells "Fuck you" and I shout back "Fuck you too".'

DYNAMITE

A man goes to the pub after work with some mates and **gets plastered**. He's feeling pretty full of himself by the time he gets home and decides he wants to have sex with his wife.

She is reading in bed when he strides in and **rips off his clothes**. 'Baby,' he growls, 'you are looking at two hundred pounds of dynamite.'

His wife jumps out of bed, flings the windows open and yells, 'Everybody **run for your lives** – there's two hundred pounds of dynamite in my bedroom with only a three inch fuse!'

HEAVEN'S GATES

Three couples have died in an accident and are waiting in line at the **Pearly Gates**. When the first couple reach the front of the queue, St Peter tells the husband, 'You're not coming in. You let alcohol rule your life and even **married a girl** called Sherry.' Disappointed, he turns and walks away.

The next couple approach St Peter who tells the husband, 'Can't let you in either, I'm afraid. You allowed money to rule your life and even married a girl named Penny.' The husband **slumps his shoulders** and walks away.

The husband of the third couple, having overheard both conversations, says to his wife, 'Come on, Fanny, he's hardly going to let us in.'

OVERWEIGHT DADDY

A little boy has a question for his mum when she picks him up from school. 'Mummy, I keep waking up to this **thumping noise** I can hear coming from your bedroom, and I go to see what it is and there you are bouncing up and down on top of Daddy. Why do you keep doing that?'

The mother is taken aback but regains her composure quickly and says, 'Daddy needs to **lose a little weight** so I bounce on him every now and again to get all the air out of him.'

Her son tells her she's wasting her time. 'That **nice looking lady** next door comes over when you're at the supermarket and just blows Daddy right back up.'

TOWEL JOB

A wealthy old man marries a stunning 20-year-old model with an insatiable sexual appetite. It soon becomes clear that the husband is not able to make her come during their **frequent sex sessions**. They decide to go to a sex counsellor.

After listening carefully to their complaint, he says that the wife might be able to come if they hire a male gigolo with a huge penis to stand naked over them during lovemaking and wave a towel at them for about ten minutes. The couple are **confused** but, willing to try anything, they do what he prescribes the next evening. Alas, the problem is not solved. They go back to the counsellor and tell him about the failure.

This time, the counsellor suggests that they get the gigolo to wave the towel for the entire period of lovemaking. They try this the very same evening, but again with **no success**. They return to the counsellor and he asks if the gigolo is waving the towel vigorously enough, as this is an important part of the therapy.

So that night the couple get down to business and tell the **gigolo** to give the towel a bloody good wave. After a few hours of lovemaking the wife has still not come. Fed up, the old man clambers off the bed, snatches the towel from the gigolo and orders him to shag his wife while he waves the towel madly. Just ten minutes later the wife reaches an **earth-shattering** orgasm, nearly breaking all the windows in the house with her piercing screams of **ecstasy**.

At this point the old man cries triumphantly at the gigolo, 'There you go, sonny – that's how you wave a fucking towel!'

Q&A

What should you do when you see your husband staggering through the door?

✦ ✦ ✦

Shoot him again.

WANT SOME OF THIS?

A middle-aged woman thinks her sex life has become a bit stale and needs **spicing up**. She goes to a sex shop and buys a pair of crotchless knickers.

That evening, she puts them on, strides up to her husband and says, 'Do you want some of this?'

He replies, 'You must **be joking** – look what it did to those knickers!'

KEEP DIGGING

An elderly couple have come to resent each other over the years and are **constantly arguing**. The old man is often heard screaming at his wife, 'I've had enough of you, you old nagging bitch! When I die, I'll dig my way out of the grave to come back and haunt you!'

He starts practising black magic and when some of the neighbourhood pets go missing, he is blamed. Days before his eighty-fifth birthday, the **old man dies**, and his wife has him put in a coffin and buried.

Later that same night, she goes to her local pub and parties like she's never **partied before**.

Her neighbour asks her, 'Don't you remember what your husband told you – that he'll dig his way out of the grave and **haunt you?**'

The old lady answers, 'Hey, let him dig 'til the cows come home. I put the coffin in upside down.'

TATTOO

A man goes into a tattoo shop and asks to have a hundred pound note **tattooed** on his penis.

The tattoo artist asks why on earth he wants that on **his member**.

The man replies that he likes to play with his money, likes to watch his **money grow** and, best of all, his wife can blow a hundred quid without even leaving the house.

IN THE DARK

A man is walking home late one night when he sees a woman **in the shadows**. 'Twenty quid,' she mumbles to him.

He's never been with a prostitute before, but he thinks 'Why not?' and the pair of them **start going at it**. Suddenly a light is pointed at them and they see a policeman.

'What's going on here, then?' asks the policeman.

'I'm making love to my wife,' the man answers.

'Oh, right, I do apologise,' says **the policeman**, 'I didn't realise.'

'Well,' says the man, 'to be honest neither did I until you shined that torch on her face.'

FLOWERS

Two women are working in an office when a big bunch of flowers is delivered for one of them from her husband.

'No doubt he'll expect me to spend the **entire weekend** on my back with my legs in the air.'

'Why?' her colleague asks. 'Don't you have a vase?'

GREAT TITS

A man is wandering aimlessly around a supermarket until he sees a **beautiful young** woman. He says to her, 'I seem to have lost my wife here in the supermarket. Would you mind talking to me for a couple of minutes?'

The woman gives him a **puzzled look**. 'Talk to you? Why?' she asks.

'Because whenever I talk to a woman with tits like yours, my wife appears out of nowhere!'

TEN HUSBANDS, STILL A VIRGIN

After divorcing ten men, a woman makes a lawyer her eleventh husband. On their wedding night, she asks him to be gentle with her as she is still a virgin. The groom is **puzzled**. 'But you've been married ten times,' he says. 'How can you still be a virgin?'

'Well, my first husband was a sales representative; he just kept telling me how great it was going to be.

'Husband number two was in IT; he wasn't sure how it was supposed to **function**, but he said he'd look into it and get back to me.

'Husband number three was in field services; he said everything checked out diagnostically but he was having trouble getting the system up.

'Husband number four was in telemarketing; he knew he had the order, but he couldn't say when he would be able to deliver.

'Husband number five was an engineer; he understood the basic process but said he would need three years to research, strategise and implement a new **state-of-the-art** method.

'Husband number six was in administration; he was pretty sure he knew how it was done, but he wasn't sure if it was really his job.

'Husband number seven was in marketing; although he had a **nice product**, he wasn't sure of the best way to position it.

'Husband number eight was a psychologist; all he ever did was talk about it.

'Husband number nine was a gynaecologist; all he did was look at it.

'Husband number ten was a stamp collector; all he ever did was... **God, I miss him**.

'But now that I've married you, I'm really excited!'

'Good,' says husband number eleven, 'but why?'

'You're a lawyer. This time I know I'll get screwed!'

GOOD FOOD

An American woman goes into a tattoo shop and tells the tattoo artist that she wants him to do a picture of a turkey on her **right thigh** just below her bikini line, and to put 'Happy Thanksgiving' underneath. Once he's done that she asks him to tattoo her **left thigh** with a picture of Santa Claus and the words 'Merry Christmas'.

The tattoos done, the woman starts getting dressed. The tattoo artist, curious, asks why she got him to put such **unusual tattoos** on her thighs.

She answers, 'I'm fed up of hearing my husband complain every year about how there's nothing good to eat between Thanksgiving and Christmas.'

TRAGIC LOVE STORY

A young man sees an old man sitting on a park bench, crying as though his heart is broken.

When the young man asks him what is wrong, the ninety-year-old **pensioner** answers through his tears, 'I've got a beautiful twenty-five-year-old wife.'

'That sounds great,' says the young man.

'You don't understand,' the old man sobs. 'We make love every morning before she goes to work. Then we **make love again** at lunchtime and afterwards she cooks my favourite meal. If she gets a break in the afternoon, she rushes home and gives me oral sex, the best an old man could ever hope for. And after supper we make love all night long.'

'I don't understand,' says the young man. 'That sounds like the **perfect relationship**. I really don't think that you've anything to cry about.'

'It's not that,' the old man wails, 'I've forgotten where I live.'

CHEATING WIVES

Three men are drowning their sorrows at a bar, each suspecting his wife of **cheating on him**.

'I found some shears and a trowel under my bed yesterday,' the first man says. 'I think my wife is sleeping with a **gardener**.'

'Well, I found a stethoscope under my bed yesterday,' says the **second man** miserably. 'I think my wife is sleeping with a doctor.'

'That's nothing,' the third man says. 'I looked under my bed yesterday and found a cowboy there. I think my wife is screwing a horse.'

ST PETER'S REWARDS

Three men are queuing up to get into Heaven. St Peter greets each of them at the gate and says, 'The vehicle you get in Heaven will reflect how well you **treated your wife**.'

When it's the first man's turn he says, 'I never cheated on my wife and I love her.' St Peter gives him a Rolls Royce and off he drives.

The second man reaches the gate and says, 'I cheated on my wife a bit but I **still love her**.' St Peter gives him a Mustang.

The next guy tells St Peter, 'I cheated on my wife a lot.' He is given a scooter.

The next day in Heaven the man who got the **scooter** is riding along and sees the man who has been given the Rolls Royce crying. He asks, 'What's the matter? You have such **a nice car**.'

The other man sniffs and says, 'My wife just passed me by on roller skates.'

YOUTHFUL BREASTS

A woman in her fifties is skipping around at home and grinning from ear to ear. Her husband is trying to read his newspaper and eventually says, 'You look **like a fool**, woman. What on earth's the matter with you?'

The woman carries on skipping and says, 'I just had a **mammogram** at the health clinic and the doctor says I have the breasts of an **18 year old**.'

Her husband says, 'Did he say anything about your 56-year-old arse?'

'No,' she replies. 'Your name never came up.'

FARMER'S WIFE

After a long day a farmer decides to have a few drinks, and ends up **pissed as a newt**.

While his wife tries to wash up the dishes from dinner, he **grabs her tits** and says, 'If these gave milk, we could get rid of the cows.' Then he **grabs her arse** and says, 'If this gave eggs, we could get rid of the chickens.'

The wife turns round and grabs the farmer's dick, saying, 'And if this stayed hard, we could get rid of your brother.'

LOVER UNCOVERED

A married woman is having an affair with a pest-control inspector. One day they are getting it on in the bedroom when suddenly they hear a key turn in the front door.

'Quick,' the woman says. 'That's my husband, he's home early. Get in there.' She hurries him into the wardrobe **stark naked**.

The husband walks into the bedroom and finds his wife in bed, although it is only the middle of the afternoon. He is immediately **suspicious** and begins to search the room. It is not long before he finds the man in the wardrobe.

'Who are you?' he asks him.

'I'm a pest exterminator from Blast-A-Bug,' the man says.

'What are you doing in my wardrobe?' the husband asks.

'I'm investigating **a complaint** about a moth infestation,' the man replies.

'And where are your clothes?'

The man looks down at himself and says, 'Those little bastards!'

PAYBACK

A man goes into a pub one night and asks the barman for a beer. 'No problem, sir,' says the barman. 'That'll be **one penny**.'

'ONE PENNY? That's brilliant!' The man can't believe his luck. He takes a look at the menu and asks, 'Could I get a nice juicy steak, with all the trimmings?'

'Of course, sir,' replies the barman, 'but now we're talking **real money**.'

'How much?' the customer asks. 'Four pence,' the barman replies. 'FOUR PENCE!'

The man is dumbstruck. 'This is the best pub I've ever been in. Where's the owner?' The barman says, 'He's upstairs **with my wife**.'

'What's he doing with your wife?' the customer asks.

The barman answers, 'Same thing I'm doing with his business.'

WORDS TO A DYING WIFE

Janet is laying on her deathbed while her husband John keeps **vigil by her side**.

With the end near, she looks up at her husband and tries to speak. 'Sweet, dear John,' she whispers.

'Hush, darling,' he says. 'You need to rest. Don't talk.'

'No, John, listen,' she insists. 'There is something I must **confess** to you.'

'There's no need, my love,' John replies gently. 'Everything's all right. You just go to sleep now.'

'No, no. I want to **die in peace**, John. I slept with your brother, your father and your best friend.'

John strokes her hair. 'It's all right, my darling Janet, I know all about it,' he says.

'You do?' she says, her voice weakening.

'Yes, I do. Why do you think I poisoned you, you slut?'

HANDY MAN

A young couple have just got married and move into their new home. One day when the husband gets in from work his wife says, 'Darling, the light in the hallway **won't work**, even with a new bulb – could you fix it?'

The husband frowns at his wife and says, 'What do I look like, Mr Wires the electrician?'

A few days later he returns after a long day in the office to another request from his wife: 'Babe, I can't get **the car to start**. Can you check it out for me?'

'What do I look like, Mr Dipstick the mechanic?' he answers.

The next week it rains non stop and his wife discovers that the roof is leaking above their bedroom. The minute he steps through the door she pleads with him: '**Sweetheart**, the roof is leaking! Please can you fix it?'

He is getting impatient now and snaps, 'What do I look like, Mr DIY?' He takes a beer out of the fridge and watches TV.

The following weekend it rains again, even more heavily this time, but the husband notices that the roof **isn't leaking** any more. He flicks the light switch on in the hall and it works, and just at that moment he hears the wife pull into the drive in her car. As she walks through the door he says, 'Honey, the roof's stopped leaking, the light works and your car seems to be running – how come?'

She replies, 'Oh, the other day I was cutting the hedge and I got chatting with one of our new neighbours, **Simon**. What a lovely man. He came round and fixed everything.'

'Brilliant! Did he charge us anything for it?' the husband asks.

'No, he said all he wanted in return was that I either bake him a **cake or shag him**,' she says.

'Cool. So what kind of cake did you make?' asks the husband.

'Cake? What do you think I look like, Delia Smith?

GOLFING BLUES

One sunny day a man and his wife play golf. They arrive at the fourteenth hole where the husband hits a huge slice that ends up behind an old barn. 'I should probably play it safe and chip it onto the fairway,' he says.

'Hang on a second,' says his wife. 'Why don't you try hitting the ball **through the barn?**' The man thinks it's worth a try. But then he slices the ball, it ricochets off the barn and slams into his wife's head. She **dies instantly**. The man is inconsolable and locks himself away for weeks in utter misery.

Eventually he realises that he must deal with his agony and heads out to the very same golf course to play. Once again he finds himself at the fourteenth hole and once again he hits a **huge slice** right behind the old barn. Just as he's squaring up to chip it safely onto the fairway, one of the other players suggests that he try and hit it through the barn.

'Oh no,' the man says, horrified. 'I tried that last time.'

'What happened?' 'I shot an eight!'

TEMPTATION TEST

Three couples want to join a church. One is an elderly couple, another middle-aged, and the other **newlyweds**. The vicar tells them that he will gladly allow them to join as long as they first abstain from sex for two whole weeks.

Two weeks later the three couples return to talk to the vicar. He asks the elderly couple if they have managed to **abstain from sex** during the last two weeks. 'Yes, no problem.' So the vicar welcomes them into his church. He asks the middle-aged couple the same question. The wife replies, 'Well, after the first week the temptation became quite strong so my husband went to bed on the couch, but we made it.' The vicar tells them that they too are welcome **in the church**.

Finally he asks the newlywed couple if they were able to control themselves for the two weeks. The husband says, 'I'm afraid not. On the third day, my wife dropped a **tin of beans** and when she bent over to pick it up, I was overcome by lust and passion.'

'I'm sorry,' the vicar says, 'but in that case I will have to ban you both from this church.'

'I understand,' says the husband. 'We're banned from Tesco too.'

THE SAVIOUR

One day little Jenny goes to play in the garden and sees her old dog Kipper on the path, **dead as a doornail** with his legs in the air. She runs back in the house and asks, 'Daddy, Daddy, why does Kipper have his legs in the air?'

Her father thinks carefully and replies, 'So that it's easier for Jesus to come and take him to heaven.'

The next day Jenny's father gets back from work and his daughter rushes up to him with some news. 'Daddy, Daddy, Mummy almost **died today**.'

Flustered, her father stutters, 'What? Tell me what happened.'

Jenny explains, 'Well, Mummy's legs were in the air and she was screaming, "Oh, Jesus, I'm coming, **I'm coming**," and if it wasn't for the milkman holding her down she might not have made it.'

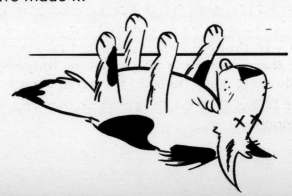

THE PERFECT HUSBAND

After a heavy workout one afternoon, several men are **getting dressed** in the changing room of a gym. A mobile phone on a bench rings and one of the men picks it up, prompting the following conversation:

'Hello?'

'Darling, it's me. Are you at the gym?'

'Yes.'

'Well, I'm in town at the moment, just looking round the shops. I've seen the most beautiful sheepskin coat. It's adorable! Darling, if you let me buy it I promise I'll give you a blow job tonight.'

'How much is it?'

'It's just £1,500.'

'OK, then, if it's that important to you, go ahead and buy it. I'll see you tonight.'

'Wait – I also happened to pass by the **Mercedes dealership** earlier and saw this year's models. There was this gorgeous silver one – you'd love it too, darling. I had a chat with the salesman and got him to give me a really good price. You will let me buy it, won't you? I'll put that **nurse outfit** on that you like so much.'

'What was the price he quoted you?'

'Only **£65,000**.'

'OK, but make sure that includes all the options.'

'Great! But hold on a second, there's just one more thing.'

'What?'

'Well, remember that house we looked at last year? The one with an acre of gardens, including a waterfall, bar complete with **games room**, indoor squash court... It's on sale!'

'How much do they want for it?'

'Only £900,000.' 'Well, all right, then, if your heart's set on it. But just bid £850,000, OK?'

'OK, darling. Thank you! See you later. I love you.'

'Bye. I love you too.'

The man **hangs up** and asks the rest of the guys in the changing room, 'Does anyone know whose phone this is?'

CLOSET TALK

A woman invites her lover to her home one morning while her husband is at work. Her cheeky 8-year-old son, who she thinks has gone to school, is hiding in her wardrobe. Suddenly the woman's husband comes home and she hears him making his way up the stairs, so she hurriedly **pushes her lover** into the wardrobe where he discovers he's not alone.

'Dark in here,' the little boy says.
The man agrees, 'Yes it is.'
Boy: 'I have a football.'
Man: 'That's nice.'
Boy: 'Want to buy it?'
Man: 'No, thanks.'
Boy: 'My dad's outside.'
Man: 'OK, how much?'
Boy: 'Two hundred and fifty pounds.'

A couple of weeks later, the boy and the mum's lover again find themselves in the **wardrobe** together.

Boy: 'Dark in here.'
Man: 'Yes, it is.'
Boy: 'I have some football boots.'

The lover, remembering their **last encounter,** asks the boy, 'How much?'

Boy: 'Seven hundred and fifty pounds.'
Man: 'Fine.'

A few days later, the boy's father says to him, 'Put your **football boots** on. Let's go outside and have a kick around.'

The boy says, 'I can't. I sold my boots and my football.'

The father asks, 'How much did you sell them for?'

The boy says, 'A thousand pounds.'

The father reprimands him. 'That's terrible, **overcharging** your friends like that. You know they didn't cost anywhere near that much. I'm taking you to church and you're going to confess.'

So they go to church and the father makes the little boy sit in the **confession booth**, closing the door behind him.

The boy says, 'Dark in here.'

The priest says, 'Don't start that shit again.'

IS THAT YOUR FINAL ANSWER?

One night, after watching *Who Wants to be a Millionaire?* on television, a man and his wife go to bed. The husband starts to get a **little frisky** with his wife until she pushes him away, saying, 'Not tonight, dear, I have a headache.'

The man says, 'Is that your **final answer**?'

'Yes,' she replies.

'OK,' he says, 'then I'd like to phone a friend.'

SEX CODE

A husband and wife use a code so they can discuss sex without their young daughter knowing what they're **talking about**. The code word is 'typing'.

One day the husband says to his daughter, 'Tell Mummy that Daddy needs to type a letter.'

The little girl passes on the message, and her mother gives her the response. 'Tell Daddy that he can't type a letter at the moment because there is a **red ribbon** in the typewriter.' The daughter dutifully goes back to her father to relay the message.

A few days later the mother says to her daughter, 'You can tell Daddy it's OK to type that letter now.'

The little girl tells her father this and is immediately sent back to her mother to report his response. 'Daddy said **no need** for the typewriter, he already wrote the letter by hand.'

THAT'S LOVE

A prisoner has served 25 years of a life sentence before managing to **escape** one night. The first thing he does is break into the home of a young couple and burst into their bedroom. They wake up, startled, and he ties the husband to a chair and the wife to the bed.

Climbing onto the bed he leans in close to the woman, who is dressed only in a thin nightie. The husband watches nervously as the intruder appears to **kiss her neck**. Then suddenly he jumps up and leaves the room in a hurry.

The husband quickly inches his way over to the bed and whispers to his wife, 'Darling, don't be scared. We'll be all right – just do whatever he asks you to. He obviously hasn't been with a woman in years and when he kissed your neck it seemed to make him pretty horny. If he wants to have **sex with you**, let him – our lives depend on it. Stay strong, darling. I love you.'

His wife finally manages to spit out the gag the escaped convict had put in her mouth. 'Sweetie, I'm so glad you feel that way. But he wasn't kissing my neck; he was whispering to me that he thought you were a real hunk and he asked if we kept the **Vaseline** in the bathroom. Stay strong, sweetie. I love you too.'

BREAST ENLARGEMENT

A couple get into bed one night.

Wife: 'I wish my **boobs were bigger**.'

Husband: 'Easy. Just rub them with toilet paper.'

Wife: 'What good would that do?'

Husband: 'It worked for your arse didn't it?'

REVENGE

A woman returns home from work early one day to find her husband in bed with his mistress.

In a **complete rage** she manages to drag her cheating husband down the stairs to the garage and put his manhood in a vice. She secures this tightly and removes the handle. While her **whimpering husband** watches, she strides over to the workbench and picks up a hacksaw.

The husband, petrified, screams, 'Stop! You're not going to cut it off, are you?'

The wife, in a **calm voice**, replies, 'No. You are. I'm going to set the garage on fire.'

KICK THE PUSSY

After being given some chores to do on the family farm, a defiant little boy storms out of the house in a huff. He heads straight for the barnyard, where he **kicks the rooster**. In a muddy pen, he kicks a pig. In the field, he kicks Daisy the cow. His mother sees all this and charges after him, fuming.

'I saw you kick the poor rooster; just for that, you'll get no eggs. And I saw you kick the pig, so **no bacon for you** either. And I saw you kick Daisy, so you'll not be getting any milk.'

The boy's father hears all the commotion and comes out of the barn to see what is going on. He immediately **trips over the cat** and, cursing, boots the miaowing creature out of his way.

The little boy looks up at his mother and says, 'Do you want to tell him or shall I?'

DRINK MONEY

Two colleagues go drinking in a nearby pub right after work. After several hours and quite a few drinks, one of the men hiccups, lets his head roll downwards and proceeds to **throw up all over himself**. He uses a clean bit of sleeve to wipe his mouth and says, 'Man, I'd better head home. I'm already really late, and now I've thrown up all over myself. The wife will not be pleased.'

His colleague turns to him and says, 'Don't worry – have you got ten quid?'

The first man checks his wallet and tells him he has.

The second man says, 'Put the note in your shirt pocket. When you get home tell your wife some bloke threw up on your shirt and he gave you a tenner for the **dry cleaning**. I do it all the time.'

The first man says, 'Great idea! Why don't we have another round,' and the two carry on drinking for another couple of hours.

Eventually they leave the pub and go their separate ways. When the first man gets home he finds his wife **waiting up** for him.

She takes one look at him and says, 'Look at the state of you! You're five hours late, you can barely stand and you've got dried puke all over your shirt! What the hell's wrong with you?'

The man remembers his colleague's advice and says, 'Listen, I can explain. **This drunk geezer** threw up on me and gave me a tenner to get my shirt dry cleaned. Honest. Check my front pocket.'

Trying to **avoid the vomit**, the man's wife reaches into his pocket and pulls out two ten pound notes. 'Hold on,' she says, 'There's twenty quid in here.'

Her husband says, 'Oh, yeah – he shat in my pants too.'

BIG BUT BRAINLESS

A family go on holiday to a sunny beach resort.

One day they visit a nudist camp and the seven-year-old daughter wanders off to collect shells. When she has collected as many as she can carry, she comes back to where her mother is sunbathing.

'Mummy,' she says, 'all the women have **bigger boobs** than you.'

Her mother tells her, 'Well, love, the bigger they are, the more stupid they are,' and the little girl goes off to find more shells.

A little while later, she comes back again with another observation. 'Mummy, all the men have **bigger willies** than Daddy.'

Her mother again tells her, 'Well, love, the bigger they are, the **more stupid** they are,' and the little girl goes off to play some more.

Later that afternoon, the little girl runs up to her mother and exclaims, 'Mummy, Mummy – Daddy's talking to a really stupid lady, and the longer he talks, the stupider he gets.'

PAGE TURNER

A couple are lying in bed. The wife turns off her bedside lamp and settles down to go to sleep, while the husband sits up and reads a book.

After a minute, he reaches his hand under the covers and starts **fondling** his wife's fanny. He does this just for a second or two before going back to his reading. A little while later he does the same again, and then once more a couple of minutes after that.

His wife becomes **aroused** and supposes her husband is waiting for some kind of encouragement before going any further. She gets out of bed, throws off her nightie and starts **dancing naked** in front of him.

Her husband looks up, confused, and asks, 'What are you doing?'

The wife replies, 'You keep playing with my fanny so I assumed you were trying to get me in the mood for making love.'

The husband says, 'No, that's not it at all.'

Now it is the wife who is **confused**. 'What on earth were you doing, then?'

'I was just wetting my fingers so I could turn the pages in my book.'

HORSE PLAY

It is Saturday morning and a man is happily reading the newspaper in peace and quiet. Suddenly his **wife creeps up** on him and whacks him over the back of the head with a frying pan. 'What was that for?' he asks, rubbing his head.

She replies, 'While I was doing the laundry I found a **piece of paper** in your trouser pocket with the name Gloria on it.'

He says, 'Oh, love, Gloria's the name of the horse I bet on at the races a couple of weeks ago.'

'Oh. Right,' she says, and gets back to the laundry.

A few days later the man is back in his chair reading the newspaper and his wife again wallops him **round the head** with the frying pan. 'Ow,' he cries. 'What's that for this time?'

She answers, 'Your horse called.'

ALSO AVAILABLE

REALLY DAFT IDEAS

D. I. SASTER

£4.99

Paperback

Some ideas should never have made it further than the half-witted minds they originated from. *Really Daft Ideas* picks out the pottiest true stories to make you laugh and cringe.

From the soldier who tied a hammock between two wall lockers, only to be fatally crushed by them at bedtime, to the man who took aim at a spider crawling up his leg and shot himself instead, this book demonstrates why it's a good idea to think before you act.

www.summersdale.com